Original title:
Life, Love, and Other Mysteries

Copyright © 2025 Creative Arts Management OÜ
All rights reserved.

Author: Gideon Barrett
ISBN HARDBACK: 978-1-80566-054-5
ISBN PAPERBACK: 978-1-80566-349-2

Whispers of the Journey

A squirrel in a tiny hat,
Plans a trip, no map, just chat.
He giggles at the wind's surprise,
As acorns fall from autumn skies.

The road is paved with peanut dreams,
And laughter bursts like bubbling streams.
He dances through the leaves so green,
In a world that's wobbly, yet so keen.

The Poetry of a Single Breath

A whisper snuck between my ribs,
Tickling thoughts like playful squibs.
Inhale the giggles, exhale the sighs,
A hiccuped rhyme beneath the skies.

A sneeze becomes a sonnet sweet,
Invisible verses, a sneaky feat.
With every breath, a chuckle grows,
In this ballet of air, who knows?

Imprints of Shared Moments

Two friends with jelly on their face,
Crack jokes about a silly race.
Each snort and snicker, tied in knots,
Like tangled strings, or baggy socks.

They share their dreams with tarts and pies,
Through whimsical tales, they truly fly.
With crumbs of laughter scattered wide,
These moments stick, no need to hide.

Fireflies in the Dark

Tiny flickers in the night,
Dancing bugs with pure delight.
They wink at wishes in disarray,
As shadows giggle and play their way.

With each soft glow, a chuckle stirs,
Mysterious secrets wrapped in purrs.
A jester's ball in the moon's embrace,
Where whimsy twirls, and time finds space.

Moments Between Shadows

In the corner, a cat snores loud,
While I fumble, feeling quite proud.
The coffee spills, a morning show,
Who knew chaos could steal the glow?

Tick-tock, a clock's broken song,
Counting minutes, what could go wrong?
A dance on the edge, a slip and a twirl,
Is it the coffee or just the world?

Whispers of the Heart

A frog croaks truths, as I sip my tea,
He claims to sing love's sweet decree.
I roll my eyes, it's quite absurd,
Yet jump if you must, you charming bird!

With mismatched socks and a goofy grin,
I navigate places I shouldn't begin.
The mirror chuckles at my wild hair,
Who put that hat on? It lost a dare!

Unraveled Threads of Time

The clock just laughed, lost its way,
With every tick, a game to play.
My socks are late, my shoes misaligned,
Oh, such mysteries my brains unwind!

A spoon's for soup, but I've got a fork,
In the kitchen, chaos starts to cork.
Mixing cupcakes with a pinch of fate,
Wondering if that's why I'm late!

The Dance of Forgotten Dreams

A waltz with laundry, a tango with dust,
I'm balancing breakfast, oh, it's a must!
Quick step around the dog's sunny spot,
In this grand ballet, I've forgot!

The moon rolls its eyes, facing the sun,
Would they ever agree that it's fun?
The stars are snickering, can't they see?
It's just a Tuesday, let me be free!

The Color of Untold Stories

In a box of crayons, bright and bold,
There lies a tale, waiting to unfold.
With swirls of laughter, and dots of glee,
Each shade a secret, just wait and see.

The red is spicy, the blue is cool,
The yellow's a joker, always plays a fool.
Green dreams of frogs, jumping high and wide,
While orange giggles, with his sunny pride.

Chasing Fleeting Moments

Time's a sneaky cat, it runs and darts,
It steals our socks and also our hearts.
We chase it with ice cream, we race with glee,
Yet it slips through fingers, oh not off a spree!

With bubblegum laughter, we dance and play,
While time rolls by in a cheeky way.
Each tick and tock, a spark of cheer,
We swing from joy, not knowing what's near.

Shadows Cast by the Moon

At night the shadows get quite a thrill,
They take to the stage, giving ghosts a chill.
With twisty shapes in a silvery light,
They waltz with the breeze and dance with delight.

The old tree chuckles as lanterns sway,
While crickets compose their night-time ballet.
A chuckle from darkness, a wink from above,
Shapes whisper secrets of ages of love.

The Pulse of Hidden Truths

In the heart of whispers, beats a sly tune,
When truths are hidden beneath the moon.
They giggle and poke behind thickened lies,
With cake made of cunning and frosting of sighs.

The hearts all giggle, as they play their game,
Truths hop like bunnies, with no sense of shame.
With each little pause, they tap dance away,
Leaving behind jokes, come join, let's play!

Moonbeams and Heartstrings

In the glow of moonlit skies,
A raccoon steals my fries,
I chase him with a puffed up chest,
This midnight snack I shall contest.

The stars giggle, they can't contain,
As my heart does a silly dance again,
We laugh at shadows, we twirl around,
In this absurdity, joy is found.

To catch a comet, what a feat,
Could use a ladder, maybe my feet,
But here I am, in my cozy chair,
Declaring war on a pizza slice affair.

So here's to the moments, bright and spry,
With laughter soaring, reaching the sky,
A wink from fate and a playful jest,
In this curious game, I feel so blessed.

The Art of Allowing

I let my socks decide their pairs,
One's striped, the other's got rare flares,
I step out boldly, a fabric parade,
Guaranteed giggles, I'm not afraid.

My cat stares like she's hit the jackpot,
As I balance cereal on my hot pot,
A brunch of chaos, a culinary joke,
Oh, how the toast sings when it's broke.

The neighbor's dog joins in for a bark,
Canines unite, igniting the dark,
We create a symphony, so bizarre,
An opera in the yard, to go far.

With every blunder, I find a smile,
Sipping my coffee, let's stay a while,
For what's the rush in this crazy spin?
Let's dance with the towers of laundry piled in.

Rivers of Uncharted Emotion

I paddled down a stream of thought,
Found a rubber duck that fate forgot,
He quacked a tune, lacking a beat,
Swam around with my sock-footed feet.

The fish chuckled, they wore tiny hats,
It's a swim meet but filled with chitchats,
A goldfish named Fred, he took the lead,
In this watery world, goofiness freed.

As bubbles rise, laughter fills the air,
Zebras on the shore start a debonair,
With rainbow sprinkles thrown overhead,
We toast to the nonsense, life is widespread.

So dip your toes in the river's flow,
Embrace the silliness, let it show,
In laughter's ripple, let's freely sail,
For every quirk is a humorous tale.

Remnants of a Forgotten Song

In the attic lies a broken tune,
A kazoo and a spoon, a musical boon,
Dust bunnies waltz as I tap my feet,
Creating a concert that's utterly sweet.

With notes that slither and jump about,
I belt a melody, with a hearty shout,
The chairs join in, they creak and sway,
On this stage of chaos, we all play.

My old guitar, it's out of tune,
Whispers secrets that make me swoon,
Yet each strum takes me to unknown lands,
Where giggles and glitter shake the sands.

So let's forget what's lost or odd,
Embrace the weirdness with a nod,
For in the remnants, life sings loud,
With every mishap, we're all so proud.

Beyond the Veil of Time

In a clock shop where seconds play,
The tick-tock dances, come what may.
A cat in a hat gives time a fuss,
While mice discuss the latest bus.

Jellybeans fall from skies of gray,
They bounce and giggle, led astray.
Eons whiz on merry-go-rounds,
Pigeons hold court with sassy sounds.

Stardust and Silhouettes

Under neon lights in a twilight haze,
Dancing shadows break into a craze.
A burger flirts with fries in a spin,
While cupcakes serenade, inviting a grin.

Socks that never match form a band,
Singing songs of your favorite jam.
They play in harmony, toe to toe,
While the coffee pot joins the show.

The Song of Untold Stories

Once a llama wore a bright pink skirt,
With every twirl, he'd dart and flirt.
Pigs on scooters zoom by with glee,
While rhymes tumble from a wise old tree.

A toaster sings the blues alone,
While butter dreams of the scone's throne.
The honeybees buzz, gossip in flight,
As frogs in tuxedos croak into night.

Threads of Destiny

In a web we weave with colors bold,
Yarn connects secrets waiting to unfold.
A squirrel in spectacles knits with flair,
Whispers of fate float in the air.

A goldfish plays chess in a glassy sea,
Making moves that puzzle even me.
The stars conspire, tossing their notes,
While rubber ducks sail on dreamboats.

Radiance of a Silent Heart

In the quiet of a crowded room,
A wink caught my eye like a balloon.
Whispers danced like shadows at play,
As time peeled back the layers of gray.

A coin slipped from my pocket with flair,
Rolling away like it didn't care.
Chasing after it, I lost my shoe,
Laughter erupted, who knew what it could do?

Notes passed like oracles through the air,
Scribbled secrets of a daring affair.
But all it read was 'do you like pie?'
Oh, the mysteries baked in a crust so sly!

With grins so wide, we danced on the floor,
Leaving behind our balance by the door.
If the heart could giggle, it surely would,
While we waltzed through the mischief of the good.

The Gift of Impermanence

A sandwich left on the windowsill,
Turns into art with an unintended thrill.
As I reached for a bite, a bird swooped low,
Guess it's sharing, not quite the show.

Tick-tock went the clock on the wall,
Pausing for a moment, then it did fall.
Time's sense of humor is often unfair,
Like my hairdo after the wild wind's dare.

Chasing sunsets with socks that don't match,
Finding joy in the oddest of patch.
Glancing at time while it tickles my toes,
Every second a puzzle that no one knows.

In folly we find our true delight,
Amid the chaos shining so bright.
With laughter our shadows grow tall,
Reminding us here, we're having a ball!

On the Edge of a Dream

Floating on clouds made of rubber bands,
I bounced my way through fleeting lands.
Upside down, I spotted a castle,
Where the reigning prince had a dreadful hassle.

His crown was a hat from a quirky store,
And his royal decree was always 'more.'
With dragons who danced on a hula hoop,
Our laughter echoed through the whimsical troupe.

Goblins would join with their tap shoes clinking,
While fairies sang tunes that kept us blinking.
Every giggle unleashed more surreal sights,
As we twirled through the delightful nights.

Waking was tough, a pull like a tease,
But I chuckled at dreams that aim to please.
On the edge, we sip magic like tea,
Knowing tomorrow, there's more to see!

Bridges Built of Hope

Planks of spaghetti cross the stream,
With meatball towers, a whimsical dream.
I dared to traverse this noodle affair,
With each step, I giggled, suspended in air.

A chef waved from the kitchen of fate,
Mixing up chance on a big dinner plate.
He winked as I balanced a fork in one hand,
While gathering smiles from all across the land.

Marshmallow clouds floated above,
In a kingdom ruled by the elder dove.
Every honk of a goose played a string,
As we danced to the tunes that joyfully sing.

In laughter we built every bridge anew,
With hopes made of jellybeans, painted in blue.
Through the silliness, this truth arises,
Connection binds us, sweetening surprises.

The Canvas of Tomorrow

With colors bright and brushes bold,
We paint our dreams, or so we're told.
A splash of joy, a dab of fear,
Each stroke's a giggle, a friendly cheer.

Once there was a cat with flair,
Who danced around without a care.
He claimed to know the secret art,
Of drawing smiles straight from the heart.

But when the colors started to run,
He found it hard to have his fun.
A masterpiece? Not quite the case,
Just a rainbow splattered all over the space.

So here we stand with canvas wide,
Let's throw some paint and take a ride.
Who knows what wonders we will discover,
In this chaotic, colorful cover?

Secrets Beneath the Stars

At midnight's hour, we gaze above,
Twinkling dots of secrets, oh how we shove.
A whisper here, a giggle there,
What's hidden out beyond this glare?

The moon's a clown in a silver suit,
Telling tales of an old galoot.
He says the stars play tricks all night,
And giggle at our silly fright.

Comets zoom with a cheeky grin,
Chasing dreams of where we've been.
Each one leaves a sparkly trail,
Of wishes granted via squirrel mail.

But wait, here comes a shooting star,
Saying, "Hey, don't wander far!"
For under this vast and open sky,
We're cosmic jesters, you and I.

Heartbeats in Harmony

Two hearts might thump a silly tune,
With rhythms that make summer feel like June.
They tap and bob in goofy time,
Syncopated giggles, oh so sublime.

One beats fast, the other slow,
Like a tortoise racing a rapping crow.
Together they move in a quirky dance,
Finding humor in each chance.

A little rhyme, a little jest,
In this silly game, they're at their best.
Who knew that pulses could create such glee?
When one heart's a drum, the other a bee.

So let's not fret when things feel offbeat,
For in this chaos, we find our seat.
With every thump, a laugh will rise,
In this tune of odd-souled ties.

The Dance of Unseen Forces

In shadows where the goofballs play,
Invisible quirks lead the way.
Gravity trips on a wobble-wobble,
Bringing giggles and playful trouble.

Time ticks in odd, silly spots,
Like a rabbit wearing polka dots.
It jumps ahead or lags behind,
In a twisty dance, we all unwind.

Energies swirl with a cheeky knott,
Trying to tell us what we ought.
But really, they're just having fun,
Making patterns where we run.

So let's embrace this goofy ballet,
Where unseen forces join the fray.
With laughter leading every chance,
This cosmic jig is our sweet romance.

Letters to the Unseen

In the mailbox sat a ghost,
Whispering secrets, the usual host.
I penned my woes, a quirky note,
    It sent me back a rubber boat.

The postman laughed as he read my plea,
"Dear invisible friend, will you reply to me?"
With ink of laughter, I wrote a pun,
Who knew the unseen could have such fun?

My stapler's missing, it must be a sign,
That staples are plotting, don't tread the line.
I'll send a letter, a humorous chase,
    For every reply is a warm embrace.

So here's to the unseen, my dear pen-pals,
In their quirky world, we're all just gals.
They ride the moon on a paper dream,
While I sip tea and draft my next meme.

A Garden of Fleeting Glances

In a patch of sun, I saw you blink,
In the garden of stares, what do you think?
A daisy stood tall, forgot its name,
And whispered to tulips, "Is this all a game?"

The bees buzzed gossip, like busy little spies,
While I tripped on daisies, oh, such clumsy lies!
You smiled at a worm, I raised a brow,
I thought we could team up, but who would allow?

A butterfly danced, in a floral race,
Over petals and stems, not a care for space.
I waved a hello, it flopped like a fool,
Which left me wondering, was I the cool?

So here's our garden, with glances so brief,
A mix of humor, with mirth and belief.
We'll laugh at the flowers, and twirl in delight,
As we capture the moments that flit out of sight.

Of Time and Tides

The clock struck twelve, with a comic sound,
Time flipped a pancake and spun around.
I asked it politely, for a minute or two,
It just giggled back, saying, "Not for you!"

The waves crashed in, with a salty grin,
Each tide dropped poetry, like fish on a spin.
I built a sandcastle, it laughed at my fate,
"Turn the tide around, don't just sit and wait!"

Seagulls were shouting, like they owned the shore,
At my fleeting moments, they begged for more.
I tossed them my sandwich, they cawed like a band,
And time, dear friend, slipped right through my hand.

So let's dance with hours, and wave to the sea,
For in these funny moments, we can just be.
With each tick and each splash, let laughter be wide,
In our journey through seconds, let joy be our guide.

The Taste of Distant Horizons

I bit into breakfast, it tasted like dreams,
A swirl of adventure, or so it seems.
As toast popped up, it grinned from the pan,
"Your day is a mystery, go, take a stand!"

With each sip of coffee, I traveled afar,
To lands of spaghetti and cheese-filled cars.
A croissant rolled over, it shared a good joke,
Told me about pastries that secretly spoke.

The jam on my biscuit had stories to tell,
Of fruit-coated journeys through flavor's bright swell.
I told it my secrets, as crumbs danced around,
In a feast of enchantments, laughter was found.

So here's to tomorrow, with breakfast in hand,
A taste of horizons, where whimsy is grand.
Let's savor the moments, make flavors collide,
In the buffet of laughter, let joy be our guide.

In the Quiet of Early Dawn

Coffee brews like magic spells,
While cats plot world domination,
Birds sing their nonsensical tunes,
As I contemplate my day's vocation.

The sun creeps up—an awkward guest,
Still tripping over moonlit dreams,
I stumble into mismatched socks,
And remind myself, or so it seems.

Toast pops up, it's a surprise!
A buttered plan gone awry again,
I swear these mismatched vibes will stick,
Like glue on fingers of children's play.

But chuckles bubble in quiet morn,
As I embrace the chaos spun,
Maybe today I'll dance with doubt,
And spin my troubles into fun.

A Time for Wings to Spread

In a garden full of oddball seeds,
Bumblebees wear tiny hats,
While daisies gossip about the breeze,
And caterpillars attempt ballet mats.

Laughter echoes through the leaves,
As butterflies misread their cues,
Twisting and twirling without care,
In a world that continues to amuse.

The sun is a bright, boisterous host,
Inviting all to join the show,
But I'm busy chasing my own feet,
In a dance I'm not ready to know.

But in this carnival of color,
Where even shadows have their say,
I'll find a way to flap my wings,
And let silliness lead the day.

The Heart's Unfolding

Underneath my pillowcase,
A treasure map of strange delights,
X marks the spot of yesterday's cake,
As my dreams unite with my bites.

I flutter through a candy maze,
Dodging gumdrops full of sass,
Chocolate rivers pull me along,
While licorice whips me with class.

Fortunes whispered from fortune cookies,
Tell of laughter in the near future,
If only I could read their gibberish,
But I'd rather enjoy the suture.

So here's a toast to all the quirks,
That make the heart a jester's throne,
In laughter's embrace, we uncloak truth,
As we treat the mundane like our own.

Silhouettes of Promise

Shadows dance on the kitchen wall,
Waltzing with the fridge's hum,
Spooning cups of empty promises,
While sporting hats—a little dumb.

I find my socks in secret places,
One's been claimed by the laundry beast,
While mismatched items share their tales,
And the toaster joins a pastry feast.

Each footprint tells a tale of mischief,
A legacy of playful sin,
Where cereal rains on Tuesday mornings,
And sleepy grins are woven thin.

But in these silhouettes of chaos,
I ponder what the end might hold,
Maybe having fun's the secret key,
To unlocking stories yet untold.

The Soundtrack of Existence

A cat on the piano, what a sight,
Playing Chopsticks with all its might.
The fish in a bowl, keeping the beat,
While the dog tap dances on two tiny feet.

The toaster sings tunes, a pop-rock show,
As crumbs form the fans, cheering in row.
A spoon and a fork, duet in the drawer,
Making sweet music, who could ask for more?

The fridge hums along, a bass so deep,
While midnight snacks beckon, tempting the sleep.
The kettle whistles a high-pitched chirp,
As I dance with my cereal like I'm in a burp!

In this quirky concert, all play their part,
Even the vacuum has rhythm and heart.
Each silly sound, a symphonic delight,
In the soundtrack of life, we dance day and night.

A Glimpse through the Fog

Through the misty morning, I trip and twirl,
Chasing elusive squirrels who do a whirl.
The coffee pot knows me, we share a glance,
In this hazy chaos, I join the dance.

Umbrellas like mushrooms, float high in the air,
People bump into each other, unaware.
A pigeon coos loudly, a villainous croon,
As I step in a puddle, just gone bananas too soon!

The fog clears up slowly, like a magician's trick,
I spy a lost sock—oh, isn't that sick?
With giggles and chuckles, I stroll through the street,
Finding joy in each stumble, my day is complete.

Life's mysteries thrive in the morning's embrace,
With laughter and clumsiness filling the space.
As I wander the pathways, both funny and odd,
I smile at the world, a true, giddy god.

Crystals in the Sunlight

Bubbles in my tea dance up to the sky,
Waving at raindrops as they float by.
The sunbeams cascade, a sparkly delight,
While my cat does yoga, oh what a sight!

Reflections of humor, on glasses that shine,
Like wizards of whimsy, all drawing a line.
A garden of colors, so vibrant and bold,
Where daisies wear tutus, all cutesy and gold.

Mirrors do giggle, as I pass them by,
Saying, "Hey buddy, you've got some pie!"
With laughter encircling each crystal thought,
Here in this madness, I find what I sought.

Through rainbows and sparkles, I shrug off the gloom,
In the realm of the quirky, the fun does bloom.
With sunlight reflecting, my spirit takes flight,
In a world made of laughter, everything's bright.

The Weight of a Whisper

When secrets are whispered, they float like a kite,
Dodging the winds, oh what a sight!
With giggles and glances, they twist and they sway,
As I tiptoe around, oh what will they say?

Each whisper carries a tickle and tease,
A message from gossip or lunching with peas.
The weight of a chuckle, like bubbles when blown,
Is heavier always than the seeds that are sown.

The whispers rush past, like leaves in a breeze,
Tickling my earlobe, making me wheeze.
With stories exchanged over cookies and milk,
Finding warmth in the laughter, as smooth as fine silk.

In the theater of chatter, I take my front seat,
With whispers like treasures, so light and so sweet.
The weight of each secret, a merry ballet,
In the rhythm of laughter, I happily stay.

When Hearts Collide

Two hearts rushed into a dance,
One tripped, while the other pranced.
Chasing after the full moon's glow,
Step on my toes? Oh, don't you know?

In the kitchen, romance brews,
Pasta boiling? Oh, what a ruse!
With every stir, we fight and fumble,
Burnt spaghetti? Just a little stumble.

With every glance, it fuels a fire,
But sometimes sparks can inspire dire.
So here we are, a comedy act,
In the circus of hearts, that's a fact!

We'll laugh at quirks and silly mistakes,
Like tripping on rugs or whining snakes.
Through every giggle, we'll find our way,
In this circus of love, we'll surely stay.

Journeys Through Uncharted Waters

Charting paths that twist and turn,
Navigating waves, hoping to learn.
The captain's hat is on a cat,
Who knew with whiskers, sailing's that?

A boat made of waffles, crew of pies,
Set sail towards candy-covered skies.
The compass spins, it's a wild ride,
And jellyfish dance, side by side.

Storm clouds gather; we all must scream,
But laughter bubbles, igniting a dream.
With every wave, we'll swim and glide,
For laughter's a sail wherever we ride.

Through hot chocolate rain and marshmallow flots,
We'll brave it all, no matter the knots.
In uncharted seas, let's laugh and sway,
With our quirky adventures, we'll find a way!

The Art of Longing

In the gallery of what-ifs and maybes,
We hang our hopes like wobbly babies.
Painted in colors outside the lines,
Every heart's a canvas, with some crazy designs.

Staring long at the clock on the wall,
Waiting for moments that seem so small.
Imagining futures with sprinkles on top,
But craving the cake? Oh, please don't stop!

Loving a joke that's older than time,
Or searching for meaning in nursery rhyme.
Every sigh thickens the plot of our dream,
Jumping at shadows, we giggle and scream.

So let's embrace this curious mess,
With all its quirks, chaos, and stress.
For in this art, we're all just trying,
To find our rhythm amidst the crying.

Beneath the Surface of Everyday

Beneath the crumbs of breakfast plates,
Lie dreams forgotten, locked in crates.
A missing sock, there's mystery we find,
Is it off with gnomes, or lost in time?

The cat plots schemes as birds take flight,
While I ponder the snacks for tonight.
With laundry masks, we spin and twirl,
In the circus of chores, oh what a whirl!

Chasing dust bunnies under the bed,
With wild imaginations in our heads.
Every mundane chore hides a surprise,
The magic of beans in a can or prize.

So let's lift the veil and smile so wide,
For in every corner, there's humor inside.
Turn dishes to treasures, each moment, we sway,
In the comedy found in the everyday.

Petals in the Breeze

Petals dance in a funky sway,
Chasing each other in bright array.
Who knew the wind was such a prank,
Turning flowers into a floral bank?

Squirrels breakdancing on a branch,
Trying to impress with a daring chance.
But trees just laugh, they've seen it all,
Nature's circus, a grand free-for-all!

Bumblebees buzzing in quirky tunes,
Jiving 'round underneath the moons.
They've got moves like no other bug,
And their dance floors smell like a honey mug.

So here we frolic, no cares to seize,
In this zany world where we catch the breeze.
With giggles galore and hearts so light,
Petals in the breeze, what a silly sight!

Reflections on a Distant Shore

Waves are gossiping, can you hear?
Shells are holding tales of cheer.
Crabs in tuxedos, they waddle by,
With dance moves that make seagulls sigh.

Sandcastles rise to a royal peak,
While little kids squeal and cheekily sneak.
Their moats hold secrets, now and then,
Tide will wash them away, to start again.

The sun doesn't set, it plays hide and seek,
While beach balls bounce, oh so unique!
Laughter erupts, splashes in the air,
At this distant shore, we care to share.

As we bask in this playful game,
No heart untouched, no soul the same.
Grab a wave, let your worries out,
The sea of joy is what it's about!

The Journey within the Echo

Step inside, the echoes call,
Who knew they'd whisper, giggle, and sprawl?
They bounce around, just like a ball,
Making this journey a playful thrall.

Shadows dance, they throw a fit,
Twirling and swirling, not giving a bit.
With every step, a chuckle streams,
Like walking through a field of silly dreams.

Mirrors reflect a curious face,
Winking back like it's a race.
Each echo giggles, "Catch me if you can!"
This journey's a riddle, a jesting plan.

So skip along, let the echoes play,
In this riddle, we'll laugh away.
A journey inward with cheeky cheer,
Unlock the mysteries, my dear!

Shadows of Yesterday

Shadows linger, but what do they say?
Creeping with secrets from yesterday.
They imitate all our silly shenanigans,
Making the mundane seem just like a dance.

Footprints of laughter, each step in line,
A parade of memories, oh so divine.
They shuffle and skip like they've lost their way,
Turning regrets into a jovial play.

With every corner, a chuckle might bloom,
As shadows make faces in every room.
They wink and they nod, a comedic chat,
Reminding us all of the humor in that.

So gather your shadows, give them a cheer,
For yesterday's quirks bring joy, my dear.
In every dark corner, there's light to be found,
Among whispers of laughter that dance all around!

Tides of Longing

Waves crash down, oh what a show,
Seagulls laugh at me below.
I chase my dreams upon the sand,
But they slip right through my hand.

A crab scuttles sideways, quite absurd,
While I'm here lost in my own word.
I build a castle, just for fun,
Then watch the tide—oh, there it runs!

The sun sets low, it's time to play,
Picnics and pranks, we'll steal the day.
With sand in my sandwich, I take a bite,
But laughter echoes in the fading light.

A Dance with the Unknown

I twirled with shadows, oh what a sight,
Stumbling over my own two feet tonight.
A partner unseen, elusive and spry,
Together we trip beneath the sky.

My socks mismatched, my hair a mess,
Yet there's joy in this clumsy excess.
A misstep here, a giggle there,
Dancing alone, do I even care?

With every turn, I lose my grip,
But oh, what fun in this fumbly trip!
In the waltz of the wild and unexpected,
Life's a dance, and I'm well-connected.

Fragments of Connection

A coffee spill, my text went wrong,
Now I'm stuck with a funky song.
The barista smirks, I laugh aloud,
In this hot mess, I feel so proud.

A friend is calling, my phone's on mute,
I wave back, she thinks I'm cute.
We wander alleys, we chase the light,
And find joy in silly, shared delight.

We're mismatched socks in a world of pairs,
Puzzle pieces with goofy glares.
In moments awkward, we find our thread,
In fragments of laughter, our hearts are fed.

Threads of an Untold Tale

Stitching stories, I weave a line,
Of quirky moments, oh how divine!
With every knot, a secret spins,
In this tapestry, laughter begins.

A rogue thread tugs at my heart's seam,
Echoes of mischief in every dream.
I quilt my fears with slips and bloops,
As the fabric of fortune entangles loops.

In this patchwork of whimsy, I find my place,
A frantic race, with a comic grace.
As stitches come loose, I simply smile,
For an untold tale is worth the while.

Thoughts in Flight

Why did the chicken cross the road?
To escape the heavy load!
With thoughts that twirl and swirl so grand,
They drift like kites across the land.

Chasing butterflies with glee,
A squirrel laughs at you and me.
With every twist, a giggle grows,
From silly hats to mismatched toes.

We ponder why the toaster's hot,
And if it has a secret plot.
While cats plan heists on sunny days,
In quest of warmth and sunlit rays.

So let your mind take airy leaps,
Where silliness in slumber keeps.
As clouds parade in skies of blue,
Just remember, they laugh at you!

The Pulse of Moments

Tick-tock says the clock on high,
But it's just the cat's sly eye.
Time dances like a floppy eel,
Winking at us with a silly feel.

A sandwich falls, we gasp in awe,
The mustard splatters chaotically raw.
With each mishap, a laugh does bloom,
Turning our kitchen into a room.

We toast to burnt and charred remains,
As laughter spills like summer rains.
With every slip a treasure found,
In moments small where joy abound.

So swing your arms and spin around,
In every heartbeat, joy is found.
For time is but a fleeting jest,
Just giggle more and forget the rest!

A Symphony of Serendipity

Listen close, the world will hum,
A tune of chaos and a beat of fun.
With socks that dance and dishes sing,
A symphony of jumbled things.

The mailman slips, the dog he flies,
As giggles burst from all nearby eyes.
With every fumble, music plays,
In perfect rhythm, life's ballet.

A spoon that's lost, a fork that twirls,
In kitchens where the laughter swirls.
As serendipity takes the lead,
We lose the cares, we plant the seed.

So hold your microphone up high,
To laughter's notes that float the sky.
In this odd concert, join the show,
For every moment helps us grow!

The Essence of Unspoken Words

What's that look, the one you give?
A hint of mischief, a cheeky sieve.
We share our thoughts without a sound,
In giggling glances, joy is found.

The wink of eyes, the curl of lips,
Silly secrets do eclipse.
In playful nudges, mischief grows,
In the silence, laughter flows.

A pat on back, a gentle shove,
Communicates a world of love.
With every pause, an inside joke,
In smiles that dance like wispy smoke.

So treasure the unspoken space,
Where laughter hides in every trace.
For in each moment, quiet and loud,
Joy blooms softly, feeling proud!

Echoes of Unspoken Wishes

In the kitchen, a dance begins,
A waltz with spatulas, flour wins.
The toaster's always on my side,
While coffee brews our quirks collide.

What secrets hide in toast's warm glow?
Burnt edges tell tales we don't know.
Two cups clink with a hopeful cheer,
The jokes we share make it all clear.

The fridge knows all our midnight snacks,
With whispers of cravings, it rarely lacks.
A sandwich made with dreams and fun,
Gravity defies — the pickle's won!

Each crumb a story, a giggle's start,
In this chaos, you have my heart.
With every bite, the laughter grows,
Echoed wishes, like windblown prose.

Secrets Beneath the Stars

On the rooftop, we pitch our tents,
In messy blankets, our laughter blends.
Stars above, like sprinkles on pie,
Every twinkle, a wink from the sky.

The moon plays jokes on our sleepy heads,
As shadows tumble in cozy beds.
Who knew the sky was such a tease?
Whispered secrets ride the midnight breeze.

A comet zips, we toss our dreams,
Roasting marshmallows, sticky seams.
S'mores and secrets, who would have thought?
In this galaxy, nothing's forgot.

With your elbow nudging, all feels just right,
Counting stars till the morning light.
The night wraps us in its silly guise,
Just a pair of misfits in truth's disguise.

The Language of Silent Glances

Across the room, our eyes collide,
A silent shout, no need to hide.
A shared snack, a hidden smile,
The language of we, in every style.

Your wink says more than words could speak,
In crowded spaces, we're quite unique.
A popcorn throw — who will it hit?
Our chuckles drown every awkward bit.

The way you roll your eyes at puns,
An unspoken bond, two silly ones.
In quiet moments, the giggles bloom,
Turning the mundane to bright costume.

In this dance of playful eyes,
Laughter wraps us like sweet surprise.
The stories shared without a sound,
In every glance, our joy is found.

Reflections in a Rain-Spattered Window

Raindrops race, like a silly game,
With each splash, they call my name.
The window's etched with nature's art,
A canvas painted with a beating heart.

Inside, we sip hot cocoa's cheer,
Watching the droplets—a view so dear.
Each bubble popping, a story told,
Our dreams overlapping like yarns of gold.

Puddle jumping in our cozy socks,
With giggles echoing, it's such a shock.
The world outside feels fresh and bright,
As we find joy in this rainy night.

Reflections dance on the glassy pane,
In this mystique, let go of the mundane.
Through jokes and warmth, we'll always see,
A splash of magic in you and me.

Echoes of Forgotten Dreams

In a world where socks go missing,
The cat is plotting schemes so dissing.
Coffee spills upon the floor,
And yet we still want to explore.

Tickling fate with feathered pens,
Chasing ducks in darkened glens.
Every laugh sparks a new delight,
As we splash through life so bright.

Maps are drawn with crayons bright,
Directions lost in morning light.
But oh, the paths we chose to tread,
Lead to snacks and silly bread.

So dance we must on wobbling feet,
With quirky hearts that never cheat.
For in this chaotic, wondrous scheme,
We find the joy in each mad dream.

Tapestry of Moments

Thread by thread, we weave our days,
In mismatched socks, in quirky ways.
Banana peels become our foes,
Yet laughter from the mishap flows.

The cat sits high on shelves of doubt,
While dogs conspire to come out.
Each tablecloth a new escape,
With spills creating stunning shape.

Tick-tock goes the clock's own dance,
While socks engage in a courtly romance.
Dancing with the dust motes bright,
We harness chaos, hold it tight.

Here's to toast that burns and sings,
To awkward hugs and silly things!
For in this fabric, rich and warm,
We find our spice, our own true charm.

Layers of the Heart

Beneath the fluff of silly jest,
A mystery's wrapped in seconds best.
We wear our quirks like comfy socks,
As joy creeps out from laughter's box.

Chasing echoes of missed romance,
In leftover pizza, there's a chance.
Spaghetti strings tie us in knots,
While laughter fills our happy spots.

A sunbeam's warm, a shadow's cold,
Each hug a story yet untold.
While googly eyes watch from afar,
Our hearts beat in a shining jar.

So let's embrace the twists and turns,
In every giggle, the spirit churns.
For in this crazy, charming art,
We find the layers of the heart.

The Puzzle of Existence

In jigsaw pieces scattered wide,
We search for meaning, take a ride.
With mismatched socks we bravely stride,
And crave the absurd with laughter applied.

Bees buzz by in bee-suited glee,
Making honey from our folly tree.
Each wrong turn a chance to play,
As reruns greet the dawning day.

Fridge magnets tell our tales so bright,
Of socks and snacks that bring delight.
While toast pops up like time on cue,
We savor moments, old and new.

So here's to puzzles, loose and wild,
To moments where we all feel like a child.
For in this game, we find our way,
With silly faces that love to stay.

An Odyssey of Echoes

In the kitchen, a chef went mad,
Chasing recipes, he looked quite sad.
Spices danced like they had a life,
His soufflé soared, then caused some strife.

A pair of socks, in a wild debate,
Arguing over who's running late.
In the dryer, they spun with glee,
Conspiring to hide and make us flee.

A cat with swagger prowls the floor,
Paws on the prowl, he plots for more.
With a flick of his tail, he claims his throne,
A kingdom made of cushions and bone.

Thus echoes roam, in laughter's wake,
Fridge magnets giggle for humor's sake.
As the odd adventures unfold and swell,
We find delight in the stories we tell.

Mosaic of Moments

A toaster popped, and what did it say?
"I'm the founder of the bread ballet!"
Crispy jumps and buttery twirls,
In the kitchen, dreams swirl like pearls.

An umbrella blooms with colors bright,
Chasing raindrops as they leap in flight.
Dancing with puddles in giddy cheer,
A splash brigade forming, loud and clear.

The goldfish swims in circles grand,
Holding court at his algae stand.
His kingdom ruled by blinks and glares,
While he's a selfie star, unaware of stares.

In this mosaic, each piece is pure,
A collage of whims, where joy is sure.
With every stitch that life extends,
We find a quirk that just transcends.

The Softness of Imperfections

A crooked picture on the wall,
Sways gently, waiting for a fall.
It smiles proudly, with a painted grin,
Whispering tales of where it's been.

The cake a tad lopsided, it seems,
Yet delicious in its sugary dreams.
Even crumbs dance when nobody's near,
Celebrating happy, without fear.

A dog with one ear flops in delight,
Howls at the moon, embracing the night.
With a wagging tail, he winks at fate,
Teaching us all to love, not hate.

In the soft shadows where humor lies,
We find the glow in imperfect skies.
Each little flaw, a reason to cheer,
Transforming the mundane, crystal clear.

Labyrinths of the Heart

A pair of sneakers, they've lost the plot,
Running in circles, like they're in a rot.
Chasing sunsets with no end in sight,
Each step a giggle, in morning light.

An old clock tickles its rusty key,
Saying, "Hurry, dear, don't wait for me!"
Time can be funny, twisting through thought,
Mocking the schemes that we all have sought.

The chairs all chatter in silly tongues,
Gossiping loudly about the young.
With every creak, they twist and tease,
In this grand theater, all find some ease.

In the maze where laughter flickers bright,
Hearts wander freely, taking flight.
Through the twists of jest, our spirits dance,
Finding joy in the oddest chance.

Flames of a Silent Flame

In the kitchen, pots collide,
Spaghetti on the ceiling, what a ride!
A burnt toast, a smoky laugh,
Dinner's gone, let's just have a bath.

Whispers of sauce, a curious dance,
Twisting and twirling, a daring chance.
But who needs forks when we can dive?
With every slip, we feel alive!

Muffin tops spill like secrets shared,
Chocolate chips fly like dreams unpaired.
Goulash giggles escape the pot,
Who knew a meal could bring such thought?

Amidst the chaos, a love that sizzles,
With every clatter, the heart just drizzles.
In this oven, our spirits combine,
An unusual dish, but oh so divine!

In the Garden of Possibilities

We planted smiles among the weeds,
Hoping they bloom into joyful seeds.
Garden gnomes giggle under the sun,
Watering cans, what an odd run!

A curious patch grows lopsided dreams,
Chasing butterflies, or so it seems.
But wait, here come the cheeky birds,
Swiping our snacks, now that's absurd!

With boots of mismatches, we stomp around,
Pulling at laughter that won't stay bound.
Every flower tells a story bright,
Of tumbles, tumbles, from day to night.

The carrots wiggle, the radishes play,
Under the moon, they dance, hooray!
Who knew soil had so much to share?
In this garden, joy fills the air!

The Symphony of Connection

Two spoons in the drawer, a comical pair,
Making sweet music, if you dare.
They clink and clatter, a joyful song,
As the kettle hums along all day long.

Juggling eggs, the clumsiness reigns,
Cracks like laughter, oh, what a gain!
Flour clouds swirl like amusing dreams,
As the batter dances, oh how it gleams!

Bananas in pajamas, a quirky sight,
Conspiring together through day and night.
Laughter spills like jelly, sticky and bright,
In this kooky kitchen, everything feels right!

Each bleep and boop, the oven's delight,
Measurements wrong but it still feels right.
With spoons as our instruments, we play on,
In this symphony, our hearts are drawn!

Chasing Fleeting Glimpses

Footsteps shuffle on the sandy shore,
Building castles with laughter galore.
Seagulls squawk secrets from way up high,
As we chase shadows that flutter by.

The waves tickle toes on a sunny spree,
Each splash a giggle, wild and free.
Collecting shells that sing of the past,
In this silly chase, we are unsurpassed!

With ice cream cones that tip and topple,
Sweet drips of joy, a messy shuffle.
Lemonade spills like dreams on the ground,
In the joy of now, true magic is found!

Chasing the sunset, we skip and twirl,
In every moment, our hearts unfurl.
Fleeting glimpses, we gather in heaps,
Turning ordinary days into giggling leaps!

The Palette of Our Days

In the morning we spill jam,
On toast like it's a canvas.
Colors of the day begin,
With coffee stains as glamour.

A dance of socks, mismatched bliss,
Partners in the laundry spin.
Whirling through the daily mess,
Finding joy where chaos wins.

The clock's a clown, it mocks our pace,
Tick-tock, a rhythmic tease.
We chase shadows in this race,
At times we fall to our knees.

With each giggle, a puzzle shifts,
The day's a riddle wrapped in fun.
We paint our moments, give them lifts,
In this masterpiece, we're one.

Meditations of the Spirit

I sat in silence, counted feet,
The ants staged a parade.
With tiny hats and tiny treats,
In nature's grand charade.

A squirrel posed like it was cool,
Daring all to bet his stash.
While pigeons played the local fool,
Dropping crumbs, a messy clash.

When thoughts get tangled, tangled tight,
I ask the moon to lend an ear.
It winks and whispers, 'Chill out, right?'
And my worries disappear.

With laughter echoing the day,
And jokes shared 'neath the stars' gleam,
We dance in this peculiar play,
And wake as if from a dream.

The Chase for Meaning

A labyrinth of socks we weave,
In search of pairs that fit.
We dig through depths of drawers to grieve,
Why all our spoons are split.

The search for answers in the fridge,
What's lurking 'neath the cake?
With leftovers that make me cringe,
A mystery, for goodness' sake.

We follow trails of chocolate crumbs,
With hope, we'll find the prize.
But end up dodging all the bums,
Who laugh and roll their eyes.

Yet in absurdity, we find,
The joy that keeps us bold.
We love the silly in our mind,
As stories weave and unfold.

Tides of Uncertainty

The weather's mood swings every hour,
A sunburn, now I'm soaked.
With rain dances that lack power,
And thunder that just joked.

We surf the waves of awkward dates,
With dinner, burned and charred.
We stumble through misguided fates,
And leave each other scarred.

Each phone call seems to drop its light,
A silent pause, a shrug.
But somehow wrong feels kind of right,
Like waiting for a hug.

We navigate this quirky tide,
With humor as our guide.
Through every twist, we still abide,
In joy and laughter, we confide.

Colors in the Margins

In the corners where crayons reside,
A moonbeam once painted a joyful slide.
Socks dancing wildly, two left feet,
Chasing rainbows while sharing a treat.

The cat wears a hat, so bold and bright,
Sipping on tea, oh what a sight!
Polka dots waltz on the walls, so free,
Mocking the frown of a grumpy old tree.

A pickle once told me a joke of yore,
It tickled the cabbage, who fell to the floor.
Lemons start laughing, a zesty parade,
While broccoli hums in a green, leafy shade.

So grab a crayon and join the fun,
The margins are wild, full of cheer and sun.
For every tickle, and giggle we've found,
Paint outside the lines, let joy abound.

Ripples of Forgotten Laughter

Down by the pond where the frogs take a nap,
A doughnut-shaped cloud maps a perfect trap.
The ducks wear sunglasses in bright, silly styles,
While turtles play poker and crack up in piles.

A dance-off ensues, with moves so absurd,
As sparrows chirp loudly, forgetting their word.
A beetle spins tales of last week's mishaps,
Where pickles and jellybeans battle in laps.

The ripples keep giggling, they tickle the reeds,
As fish start to bubble with playful misdeeds.
"Why did the crab cross the road?" one fish cries,
"To get to the other side, oh what a surprise!"

With laughter a echo, they all start to sway,
The pond's little secrets keep boredom at bay.
Wave after wave, let all worries flee,
Join in the fun of this whimsical spree!

The Essence of a Breath

In the morning, a yawn like a lion's roar,
It bounces around as it flops on the floor.
A sneeze comes along, sends a cat in a spin,
Who lands on the couch with a flick of its chin.

The smell of pancakes wafts through the air,
A syrupy river, it's everyone's share.
Butterflies giggle, trapped in a jar,
While ants make a band, oh how bizarre!

A deep breath in, let the giggles begin,
As bubbles float out from the laugh of a grin.
The scent of warm cookies begs all to partake,
But cupcakes rebel, shouting, "For goodness' sake!"

And as the sun dips, casting shadows so wide,
The breath of the night collects secrets inside.
With each little whisper, a chuckle's been bred,
Life's greatest mysteries dance round in our head.

Beneath the Canopy of Dreams

Under the trees where the whispers run free,
A raccoon once tried to climb up a bee.
With pockets of acorns and shoes made of foam,
They fashioned a wagon to transport their home.

A breeze carried secrets, tickling leaves,
While a squirrel with manners insisted on cleaves.
The sky wore a blanket of oranges, pinks,
As a busy old owl juggled tiny old drinks.

"Who moved my cheese?" asked a curious mouse,
"Not I!" said a toaster, "I'm stuck in this house!"
The shadows all chuckled, creating a scene,
Where dreams danced together, silent but keen.

So gather your giggles, let worries float high,
Under this canopy, all dreams can fly.
With every odd thought that we manage to weave,
We find in the jest, a reason to believe.

Starlit Promises

Beneath a sky of twinkling sights,
We dance like fools on summer nights.
With ice cream drips and silly games,
We laugh and shout, forget our names.

The moon can be our trusty guide,
We'll hide our fears and take a ride.
A sandwich here, a cookie there,
Let's toast to chaos in the air.

Whispers of dreams on cotton clouds,
We'll spin our tales, stand out from crowds.
Where every hiccup's just a spark,
We're glowing bright, we'll leave a mark.

So stash your worries, let them stew,
Embrace the odd, the untried too.
With every loop, a joke unfolds,
And starlit secrets we will hold.

Fragments of a Delicate Tapestry

In every thread, a story hums,
Of tangles tight and silly drums.
From mismatched socks to coffee spills,
We weave our joys and random thrills.

A patch of laughter stitched with care,
A failed soufflé with lemon flare.
We'll paint this quilt with vibrant hues,
A canvas filled with quirky views.

Each little mishap, a tiny gem,
We gather like confetti, them!
With buttons lost and stains that cling,
We'll wear the chaos like a king.

So lift a glass to tangled fate,
And all the quirks we celebrate.
In every flaw, a chance to shine,
We'll toast to joys forever mine.

Enigmas in the Quiet Hours

At midnight's hour, strange thoughts parade,
Why do socks vanish? Who has it made?
The mysteries lurk in shadows near,
With Gummy Bears, our greatest fear.

The clock ticks on, it laughs and sighs,
While cereal drowns in milk goodbye.
Does toast burn brighter in the night?
These questions keep me up till light.

Cats plot their schemes with graceful grace,
While I search for my other shoe's place.
With giggles lost in bedtime tales,
These quiet hours win with quirk and scales.

So let them dance, these thoughts so wild,
A sleepy brain is just a child,
Forever pondering the absurd,
In whispered secrets, truths unheard.

A Symphony of Solitude

In a room where silence softly plays,
I twirl with dust in cozy bays.
The lonely chair begins to hum,
With echoes from the fridge's drum.

Each cereal box, my only friend,
We share our secrets and pretend.
The sock puppet murmurs soft with glee,
While houseplants nod, they're rooting for me.

Mondays crash with grand clichés,
And Tuesdays shuffle, looking dazed.
But every glance at the empty space,
Unveils a dance, a quiet grace.

So here I am, with quirks on stage,
A solo act, a favored page.
In solitude's embrace, I thrive,
With laughter echoing, I am alive.

A World in the Balance

A cat in a hat, what a sight,
Balancing dreams with all her might.
Sipping tea with a twist of fate,
Wondering if it's too early to wait.

A spoon on the floor, it starts to dance,
To a tune of chance in a fanciful trance.
Ducks in a pond, they quack and slide,
In this crazy world, we let giggles ride.

The juggler grins at the crowd so see,
Balls flying high, near a buzzing bee.
He drops one in soup, the audience cheers,
A laugh, a splash, it's all in jeers!

Tomorrow's fortune in a fortune cookie,
But all it said was, "Don't be a rookie."
With eggs on your face and dreams in your toes,
Life's a circus, it's fun, it just grows.

The Winding Path Ahead

On paths all tangled with wild delight,
You trip on your shoelace but laugh at the sight.
Pine trees whisper secrets to the squirrels,
While the sun throws its light, and the world twirls.

Kites tangle in branches, a dance good and free,
A tumble down hill spills both giggles and glee.
Unexpected rocks challenge the fleet,
"Who put that there?" as you stumble on feet.

But out from the bushes, a sandwich appears,
Plastic-wrapped dreams bring the hunger to tears.
As ants join the party, the adventure unfolds,
Each crumb a new chapter, a treasure retold.

Serendipity in Stillness

In silence, a tap from a shoe on the floor,
Reminds us of rhythms we can't quite ignore.
A snail tries to salsa, a tortoise joins in,
Groovin' through gardens, they twirl with a grin.

The fountain laughs back, with splashes of flair,
As sunlight joins, it twinkles, it's rare.
Missed the Monday meeting—what a grand mess,
But your cat walked on keys, and now you confess!

A moment of grace, with a tea-bag that's lost,
Frogs on a lily pad laughing at frost.
In stillness, we find all the giggles await,
It seems the best chaos, is often just fate.

www.ingramcontent.com/pod-product-compliance
Lightning Source LLC
Chambersburg PA
CBHW071842160426
43209CB00003B/384

The Language of Unsaid Words

In whispers of glance, she rolled her eyes,
He laughs in return, no need for disguise.
A nod and a wiggle, foreplay in mirth,
The joy of the quiet, too loud for its worth.

A pizza too cold goes unaddressed,
Yet laughter erupts, for this is the best.
Words stuck in traffic, thoughts out for a stroll,
In the space between lines, we all find our roll.

A knowing smile, the glance of a friend,
The quiet that lingers, no need to pretend.
Unsaid and unsung, in a rhythm they dance,
In a world full of madness, enjoy the romance.